I0165033

The Big Picture
~ Restoration of Relationship ~

A Short Study
of
the Bible

by
Al and Jere Litchenburg

THE BIG PICTURE

Copyright © 2014, 2018, 2020
by Al and Jere Litchenburg

All rights reserved. No part of this book may be reproduced in any form or by any electronic or mechanical means without the express written permission of the authors.

Except where indicated otherwise, all Scripture quotations in this book are taken from the New American Standard Bible®, ©1960, 1962, 1963, 1968, 1971, 1972, 1973, 1975, 1977, 1995 by The Lockman Foundation. Used by permission. www. Lockman.org

Printed in the United States of America.

ISBN: 978-1-7339955-9-7

For information, contact the authors:

info@bible-bigpicture.com

www.bible-big picture.com

Published by:

Chilidog Press LLC
pbronson@chilidogpress.com

Chilidog Press
Loveland, Ohio
www.chilidogpress.com

Book design by Andy Melchers

WHAT READERS ARE SAYING ABOUT
THE BIG PICTURE

"*The Big Picture* will bless people of all ages and walks of life! Three generations of my family have been impacted by this incredible book—my young son, myself and my mother. Just like God's Holy Word, this gem met each of us where we were and touched our hearts with the message we needed. Here at NSO, we have been distributing it to our homeless brothers and sisters. Regardless of where they are in their walk with God, *The Big Picture* brings understanding, peace and hope. My advice: Drop everything and read this book now—then pass it on!"
—Stacey Ninness, President and CEO, Neighborhood Services Organization, Oklahoma City

"*The Big Picture* provides an easy-to-read and understand foundation for belief in God's gift of Himself to mankind. The death and resurrection of Jesus provides us with the ability to reunite with our God of love for eternity. This book, which can be read in a short amount of time, sets the stage for unbelievers, novice believers and mature Christians to understand why God created us, loves us and wants us to eternally celebrate life with Him. This writing is a 'must read' to understand salvation."
—John Schille, business executive

"This powerful little book condenses the 66 books of the Bible into an easy-to-grasp 'big picture' of God revealing Himself to us and His plan to restore His relationship with us. It ties together prominent persons and events in the Bible and answers many questions the reader may have, whether new to the Bible or far along in their faith journey."
—Pete Weaver, business executive

"Al and Jere Litchenburg have been longtime supporters of The Children's Center Rehabilitation Hospital, founded in 1898 by Ms. Mattie Mallory. One of Mattie's most famous quotes states, 'We need a simple faith that takes God at His word.' And this is precisely what Al and Jere demonstrate in *The Big Picture*. Their book provides an overview of Christ's plan for our lives and helps us understand the marvel of God's great, unconditional love for each of us. As CEO of The Children's Center Rehabilitation Hospital for the past 42 years, and now Executive Chairman, I have given this book to countless people going through some of the most challenging times in their lives. It has served as a comfort to them and has helped them develop 'A simple faith that takes God at His word.' I wholeheartedly recommend *The Big Picture* for anyone seeking a simple faith and understanding of God's plan for their life. Thank you, Al and Jere, for everything you have done for The Children's Center Rehabilitation Hospital and for writing this book which has impacted so many."
—**Albert Gray, Executive Chairman of the Board of Directors**

"*The Big Picture* is easy to read and perfectly fills the gap between a Bible tract and the Bible itself. It first presents an overview of the Bible and its main message, and ends with an opportunity to accept the great gift God is offering."
—**Tony Satterfield, Director, APL Insurance Company**

"The idea of simply sitting down and reading the Bible can oftentimes be intimidating and confusing, especially for the vast number of people who have had little to no Bible study experience. *The Big Picture*, with its simple construction, may be a great first step for these folks. Getting the whole story in a synopsis is a great start and can only lead those who may otherwise fail on their own to say, "Oh, now I see how this all fits together—I want to read more!"
—**Mike Bryan, business executive**

"The Holy Spirit strongly touched the author of this wonderful book, me, and three precious brothers to begin diligently studying the Bible. We got together at least weekly to study, test one another and let the Holy Spirit teach us for well over 20 years. I can sincerely tell you that Al is one of the best men I've ever known and the most knowledgeable in understanding the real truths of the precious Gospel! May God bless the readers of this book."
—**Dave Moore, business executive**

"I have spent the last 34 years with a ministry focused on apologetics and evangelism. I am constantly looking for effective tools and *The Big Picture* by Al and Jere Litchenburg qualifies. I am anxious to get it into the hands of those for whom it will make an eternal difference."
—**Ken Mendenhall, Area Director, Search Ministries, Oklahoma City**

"In today's fast-paced world, our learning and belief systems have increasingly been shaped by media, which relies on attention-getting headlines and intentionally short 'sound bites,' often taken out of context from the more complete narrative. The truth is often elusive. For many, the Bible is often viewed as a complex and overwhelming compilation of Jewish history, the story of Jesus and his teachings, and various letters from his followers. As a result, its essential message is too often unexplored or not understood. In this light, *The Big Picture: Restoration of Relationship* provides an inspired, compelling and essential message that will invite deeper investigation of God's purpose in His creation and His plan for our lives. I encourage everyone to read this little book. The truth of the Bible is presented in clear, concise and compelling simplicity. Once you get 'the big picture,' you'll want to dig deeper. It will change your life."
–**Bruce Stover, business executive and founder of The 4th Quarter**

"I was privileged to meet Al about 20 years ago at an industry event. It was amazing how quickly we connected and I was impressed with his ability to take some very complicated issues and break them down to concepts that all could understand. His book explains how one can truly have forgiveness and hope. It is a subject that we all need to understand and continue learning. *The Big Picture* will help you on your journey and is a must read."
—**James P. Rousey, business executive and author of *Called To Care***

"*The Big Picture* is simple, concise and easy to read. It is a great overview of God's Word. People who might not read the Bible itself can read this and learn about God's wonderful plan for us. I pray that it will be used to further His kingdom."
—**Bob Willingham, business executive**

DEDICATION

This book is dedicated to our kids, grandkids and family, all of whom have come to know and love the Lord. We are so proud of each and every one of them.

ACKNOWLEDGMENTS

God deserves all the credit for inspiring the writing of *The Big Picture.* We would like to thank our ASTC (Abundance Shared through Christ) brothers who helped us learn the Scriptures and grow in Christ through weekly Bible studies that began in 1981: Dave, Pete, John and Glenn. Finally, we are thankful for our friend and Bible teacher, Ken, and our daughter, Lisa, for providing editing and other valuable suggestions.

Christian Cross in the Sunset © Can Stock Photo/phila54
Open Holy Bible on a Table © Can Stock Photo/Christian Chan

CONTENTS

CONTENTS

12

Foreword

The Big Picture is a *powerful* little book, giving readers a quick look into how the overarching story of the Bible fits together. Having a goal to read the Bible cover-to-cover can be daunting, but this book explains some of the most important concepts of the Bible in a very easy and understandable way for all. It can reintroduce lifelong believers to beloved characters included in every Sunday School class, but is also the perfect way to share the Gospel (good news) with someone who may be new to the Bible. It does a great job keeping it simple while still telling the story of our relationship with Christ. It helps us understand just how much God loves us—His children—completely and unconditionally. Love, hope and relationship… it's all part of His master plan, and this book explains it in a very easy way, using scripture references in every chapter.

Often, we skip through the parts of God's Word that are hard to understand or don't seem as relatable to us today, but *The Big Picture* makes it possible to link the stories together, increasing our desire and understanding for the story at large. While not a substitute for the Bible itself, this book walks the reader through the fundamentals of Christianity and God's divine plan, and also helps create an outline for all who wish to study the Bible but may be unsure where to start.

This book is so easy to read and helps us understand the message of the Bible in a simple way. God's plan is made clear through the simplicity of *The Big Picture*. It is the perfect book to have at home or to give as a gift because it can be read and understood by anyone. It's an awesome resource to use to meditate on scripture and allow the Word of God to reign in your heart. Its versatility makes it the perfect resource for Sunday School groups, outreach organizations or new believers. It encourages us to use the Bible as the ultimate source of knowledge. This little book answers the most foundational questions about Christianity in an accessible way for readers of all ages!

Kids, grandkids & family of
Al and Jere Litchenburg

October 2020

Introduction

The Bible can be summed up in just three words:

Restoration of Relationship

It is all about man breaking his fellowship with God, and as a Father would do, God bringing us back into a right relationship with Him. We were not capable of doing this ourselves, only God could do it. With His "love" nature, God's desire was to forgive us; but He is also "just," and therefore needed a lawful way to do it. So He came to us in the person of Jesus Christ to take all our sins upon Himself. Through the Cross, He paid the just penalty for our sins so that we could be reconciled and live forever with Him. This is why the message of the Bible is called the *Good News*! Through Jesus' birth, life, death and resurrection, our relationship with God has been restored!

The purpose behind the creation of *The Big Picture* is to give an overview of the Bible that can be read in a short amount of time. This is not a substitute for reading the Bible itself; however, if you understand the "big picture" of what the Bible is communicating to us, then it should help your reading and understanding of the real thing. Through Bible studies with fellow Christians, the following is what we believe the Bible teaches. We want to share the *Good News* with our family, friends and others while there is still time. The Bible tells us that God is Love and that He is patient and kind, not wanting anyone to perish but that everyone should come to a knowledge of the truth, repent of their sins and accept the gift of eternal life through His Son.

The Bible teaches us that we have a Savior whose name is Jesus. He is the only one who can help us because He has already paid the price to restore our relationship with God. Now it's up to each one of us to accept or reject the gift He is offering. Our prayer is that *The Big Picture* will help you and others have a better understanding of His divine plan and a closer walk with Him.

2 Corinthians 5:18-21

18 Now all *these* things are from God, who reconciled us to Himself through Christ and gave us the ministry of reconciliation, 19 namely, that God was in Christ reconciling the world to Himself, not counting their trespasses against them, and He has committed to us the word of reconciliation. 20 Therefore, we are ambassadors for Christ, as though God were making an appeal through us; we beg you on behalf of Christ, be reconciled to God. 21 He made Him who knew no sin *to be* sin on our behalf, so that we might become the righteousness of God in Him.

2 Peter 3:9

The Lord is not slow about His promise, as some count slowness, but is patient toward you, not wishing for any to perish but for all to come to repentance.

CHAPTER 1

In The Beginning

From Genesis to Revelation, the theme of the Bible is "restoration of relationship." From the very beginning, God's fellowship with man was broken because of sin. In order to restore us to His own, we had to be brought near to Him again. Genesis 1:1-2 tells us that in the beginning, God created the Heavens and the Earth, and the Earth was formless and void because it was covered with water. So He (the Spirit of God) moved over the waters and the process began toward the formation of the Earth that we inhabit today. Scientists say that the Earth is millions of years old and that could be true. God created the Earth "in the beginning" and then perhaps many years later, even millions of years, He "moved over the waters."

Some have raised the question as to the actual measure of a "day" as used in the Bible. Were the days in 24-hour segments? They certainly could have been, but it really doesn't matter. The creation story can be true either way and be consistent with what we observe in nature and scientific discovery.

Genesis 1 and also John 1 say, "In the beginning…" Let's look at John 1:1-3 & 14. "In the beginning, the Word was with God and the Word was God … and the Word was made flesh and dwelt among us." Who is referred to as the *Word*? Verse 14 makes it clear the *Word* is Jesus. What the Bible is saying is that Jesus was with God in the beginning! Jesus is the *Word* of God, so when we take the two scriptures together we have a reference to the Trinity: God (the Father), Spirit of God (moving over the waters), and the Word of God (Jesus). It is important to realize that Jesus didn't just come into being when he was born in Bethlehem. He already existed as God but came to Earth to take on human form at the appointed time.

Genesis 1:1-2

1 In the beginning God created the heavens and the earth. 2 The earth was formless and void, and darkness was over the surface of the deep, and the Spirit of God was moving over the surface of the waters.

John 1:1-3, 14

1 In the beginning was the Word, and the Word was with God, and the Word was God. 2 He was in the beginning with God. 3 All things came into being through Him, and apart from Him nothing came into being that has come into being. 14 And the Word became flesh, and dwelt among us, and we saw His glory, glory as of the only begotten from the Father, full of grace and truth.

Discussion Questions

1. How old is the Earth? What does science say, and what does the Bible say? How do we reconcile the two?

2. Did God create the world in 24-hour days, or was there some other measure for a day back then? Does this matter? Why or why not?

3. Who is Jesus and when did He come into being? How do we know this?

4. What is Jesus called in John 1? How does this relate to the creation story?

5. What power did God use to create everything we see? How can this be?

NOTES

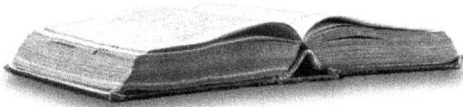

CHAPTER 2

Adam and Eve

On the sixth day, God created all the land animals after their own kind. Then, for His crowning achievement, God created man, first Adam and then Eve. God knew that it was not good for man to be alone, and so out of the side of Adam, Eve was formed as a companion and helpmate. The Bible also says that when a man and woman get married they become one flesh. We believe Adam and Eve were real people and God created them just as the Bible says. We always use the Golden Rule of Biblical Interpretation, which says, "When the plain sense of Scripture makes common sense, seek no other sense; therefore, take every word, at its primary, ordinary, usual, literal meaning unless the facts of the immediate context, studied in the light of related passages and axiomatic and fundamental truths, indicate clearly otherwise."

The Garden of Eden was a paradise created just for Adam and Eve. God created man so that He might have fellowship with us. Just as any Father would hope, God wanted Adam and Eve to have a relationship with Him based on their own free will. So God gave Adam and Eve the ability to make their own choices and willingly follow His instruction. To love God freely meant there would need to be a choice *not* to love and follow God. So Adam and Eve were created in God's image and likeness. They loved and walked with God, but were tempted and gave in to sin—first Eve and then Adam. Satan (the devil, or Lucifer) came to them in the form of a creature, a serpent, because he was a spirit being and needed a physical form. He was the one who provided the temptation.

Genesis 2:18, 21-22

18 Then the Lord God said, "It is not good for the man to be alone; I will make him a helper suitable for him." 21 So the Lord God caused a deep sleep to fall upon the man, and he slept; then He took one of his ribs and closed up the flesh at that place. 22 The Lord God fashioned into a woman the rib which He had taken from the man, and brought her to the man.

John 8:44

You are of your father the devil, and you want to do the desires of your father. He was a murderer from the beginning, and does not stand in the truth because there is no truth in him. Whenever he speaks a lie, he speaks from his own nature, for he is a liar and the father of lies.

John 10:10

The thief comes only to steal and kill and destroy; I came that they may have life, and have *it* abundantly.

Isaiah 14:12-14

12 How you are fallen from heaven, O Lucifer, son of the morning! How you are cut down to the ground, you who weakened the nations! 13 For you have said in your heart:'I will ascend into heaven,

I will exalt my throne above the stars of God; I will also sit on the mount of the congregation On the farthest sides of the north; 14 I will ascend above the heights of the clouds, I will be like the Most High.' (NKJV)

Discussion Questions

1. What is the "Golden Rule of Biblical Interpretation?" Why is it important to know how to interpret the Bible?

2. On what day did God create Adam, and why did He create Eve?

3. What was the Garden of Eden?

4. Why did God create man with free will? What would be the alternative?

5. Who tempted Adam and Eve to sin and disobey God? In what form did he appear to them? Who exactly is this tempter and how did he come into existence?

NOTES

_____

_____

_____

_____

_____

_____

_____

_____

_____

_____

_____

_____

_____

_____

CHAPTER 3

Cain and Abel

After Adam and Eve disobeyed God, there were severe consequences. They were expelled from the Garden of Eden so that they might not eat of the Tree of Life and live forever. They received a just sentence for their disobedience and the Earth itself was cursed. In this condition, God knew that man would need a Savior. His first promise of a Savior was in Genesis 3:15, where He said the seed of woman (Jesus) would bruise the head of the seed of man (Satan), and his head would bruise Jesus' heel.

After this, Cain and Abel were born to Adam and Eve. Both sons were asked to bring a gift to God from the first fruits of their labor. Abel was a shepherd, so he brought his best lamb and that pleased God. Cain was a farmer but he did not bring his best produce. God was not pleased and Cain became angry. God gave him a chance to repent but instead, his anger and jealously overcame him and he rose up and killed Abel. This was the first murder and physical death on the Earth. Thus, Abel became the first person martyred for his faith. God banished Cain from the land of Eden and he became a wanderer. Adam and Eve did have other children, one of which was Seth. He is the son through which we eventually came. From the line of Seth there were many descendants, including a man named Noah. At Noah's time in history, there was such a deterioration in man that God had to take extreme measures. The original sin (man's disobedience in the garden) started the decline. God told Adam and Eve that if they ate from the fruit of the "tree of the knowledge of good and evil," they would surely die. God was not talking about physical death but instead, *spiritual death*. Their relationship with God suffered and there was now a separation in their communion with God. The correct translation of what God said is this: "In dying you shall die," which means, in dying spiritually you shall eventually die physically.

Genesis 3:15

And I will put enmity between you and the woman, and between your seed and her seed; He shall bruise you on the head, and you shall bruise him on the heel.

Genesis 4:8-10

8 Cain told Abel his brother. And it came about when they were in the field, that Cain rose up against Abel his brother and killed him. 9 Then the Lord said to Cain, "Where is Abel your brother?" And he said, "I do not know. Am I my brother's keeper?" 10 He said, "What have you done? The voice of your brother's blood is crying to Me from the ground."

Genesis 2:16-17

16 The Lord God commanded the man, saying, "From any tree of the garden you may eat freely; 17 but from the tree of the knowledge of good and evil you shall not eat, for in the day that you eat from it you will surely die."

Discussion Questions

1. What were the consequences of Adam and Eve's disobedience?

2. Where in the Bible is the first promise of a Savior, and what does it say?

3. What children were born to Adam and Eve, and what happened to them?

4. Why was God not pleased with Cain's gift?

5. When God told Adam and Eve they would surely die if they ate from the "tree of the knowledge of good and evil," what did He mean?

NOTES

_____

_____

_____

_____

_____

_____

_____

_____

_____

_____

_____

_____

_____

_____

_____

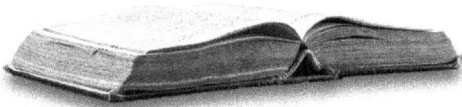

CHAPTER 4

Noah and The Flood

Sin reigned throughout history and culminating with Noah's generation, there were only a few people left with any measure of regard for God. It was Noah and his family. One theory says that it was necessary for God to cause the flood, for if Noah's family had continued to exist with unbelievers, they would have eventually been corrupted themselves. That would have ended the righteous line through which Jesus would come. When we use the word "righteous," we are not saying that we never do anything wrong. It simply means we believe God and want to follow Him and try to do what's right. So, Noah and his family were the only righteous people left on Earth. It was therefore necessary to preserve the righteous line (through Noah and his family) until time for Jesus to come.

Noah did exactly as God instructed and built an ark (a large boat) that saved all his family (Noah, his wife, three sons and their wives), along with two of every species of living creatures (male and female). The dimensions of the ark are given in the Bible. It was 450 feet long with three levels. After the floodwaters receded, the ark came to rest on Mt. Ararat in present-day Turkey. God blessed Noah and his family to repopulate the Earth and made a covenant to never again bring a flood on the Earth to destroy the human race. The sign of the covenant is a rainbow in the sky.

The three sons of Noah were Shem, Ham and Japheth. The righteous line was preserved and Jesus (and the Jewish people) descended from Shem. It is believed the people of Africa and some parts of Asia descended from Ham, and the people of Europe and other parts of Asia descended from Japheth.

Genesis 7:7-10, 23

7 Then Noah and his sons and his wife and his sons' wives with him entered the ark because of the water of the flood. 8 Of clean animals and animals that are not clean and birds and everything that creeps on the ground, 9 there went into the ark to Noah by twos, male and female, as God had commanded Noah. 10 It came about after the seven days, that the water of the flood came upon the earth. 23 Thus He blotted out every living thing that was upon the face of the land, from man to animals to creeping things and to birds of the sky, and they were blotted out from the earth; and only Noah was left, together with those that were with him in the ark.

Genesis 9:14-15

14 It shall come about, when I bring a cloud over the earth, that the bow will be seen in the cloud, 15 and I will remember My covenant, which is between Me and you and every living creature of all flesh; and never again shall the water become a flood to destroy all flesh.

Discussion Questions

1. What is meant by the word "righteous," and what is the righteous line?

2. Why did God destroy so many people in the Flood?

3. Who were the righteous people on the Earth during Noah's time?

4. What is the sign of the covenant God made with Noah and all living creatures, and what does it mean?

5. Who descended from Noah's son, Shem? What about Ham? Who came from Japheth?

NOTES

CHAPTER 5

Abraham and Isaac

As we go further in the Bible, we encounter a man named Abraham. God called Abraham out of his homeland to a place that He would show him—the Promised Land. This is the beginning of Israel and the Jewish people. God chose Abraham to be the father of the Jewish nation, and made a covenant with him. The sign of the covenant was circumcision. God promised him a son and many descendants. Abraham's wife, Sarah, was very unsure how the promise of a son through her would be fulfilled since she was very old at the time. So she had Abraham father a son with her handmaiden (servant). He was named Ishmael and he became the father of the Arab people.

God had a plan for Abraham and Sarah, though, and He was faithful to fulfill it. At age 90, Sarah bore a son who was named Isaac. As Isaac grew into boyhood, God asked Abraham to offer him as a sacrifice on a particular mountain (where it is believed the Temple Mount in Jerusalem is today). Abraham followed God's command and took him to the mountain. He believed that if God allowed the sacrifice, then God would raise Isaac from the dead and restore him to Abraham. Why? Since God had promised Abraham many descendants *through Isaac*, Abraham believed God would fulfill that promise.

The Bible says that Abraham believed God and it was credited to him as righteousness. In the biblical account, we see that a ram was provided as a substitute. This is an example of what God would later do. He would offer a sacrifice of His own son, Jesus, as our substitute.

Hebrews 11:8

By faith Abraham, when he was called, obeyed by going out to a place which he was to receive for an inheritance; and he went out, not knowing where he was going.

Genesis 15:5-6

5 And He took him outside and said, "Now look toward the heavens, and count the stars, if you are able to count them." And He said to him, "So shall your descendants be." 6 Then he believed in the Lord; and He reckoned it to him as righteousness.

Hebrews 11:17-19

17 By faith Abraham, when he was tested, offered up Isaac, and he who had received the promises was offering up his only begotten *son*; 18 *it was he* to whom it was said, "In Isaac your descendants shall be called." 19 He considered that God is able to raise *people* even from the dead, from which he also received him back as a type.

Discussion Questions

1. Who was Abraham and what nation did he father?

2. What did God promise Abraham and what was the sign of their covenant?

3. Who was Abraham's promised son and what were the circumstances of his birth? Who was born before him, and what nation did he father?

4. Why was Abraham willing to sacrifice his son, Isaac?

5. A ram was provided as a substitute for Isaac. Who was provided as a substitute for us? What does this mean to you?

NOTES

_____

_____

_____

_____

_____

_____

_____

_____

_____

_____

_____

_____

_____

_____

CHAPTER 6

Jacob and Joseph

Isaac was in the righteous line, and so was his son, Jacob. Through Jacob 12 sons were born, and they and their descendants became the 12 tribes of Israel. Jacob is also called Israel. In the son Judah, we have the line through which Jesus came. From the son of Levi came all the Jewish priests. The youngest son was named Benjamin. One of the 12 was Joseph. All of his brothers, except Benjamin, resented Joseph because they felt he was their father's favorite. They faked his death, but actually sold Joseph into slavery. He was taken away to Egypt, but the brothers told their father that Joseph was dead. Through it all, Joseph continued to trust God. He would say that his brothers meant his slavery for evil but God meant it for good.

When Joseph was sold into slavery in Egypt, he became a house servant and was highly trusted. However, after rejecting the advances of his master's wife, he was falsely accused by her of an indiscretion and was imprisoned. After years of confinement, he was called on to interpret a dream that the King of Egypt, the Pharaoh, had. His interpretation was correct, and Joseph became favored by Pharaoh and was made second in command to him. Joseph had predicted a time of plenty and a time of famine, and he told the ruler of Egypt how to plan for both. Joseph's family came to Egypt during the famine in search of grain to buy. Through God's plan, Joseph was reunited with his family and they came to live in Egypt and multiplied. Over time, their numbers grew so large that a new Pharaoh became concerned that they would rebel, so all were made slaves.

Genesis 32:27-28

27 So he said to him, "What is your name?" And he said, "Jacob." 28 He said, "Your name shall no longer be Jacob, but Israel; for you have striven with God and with men and have prevailed."

Genesis 41:15-16, 39-41

15 Pharaoh said to Joseph, "I have had a dream, but no one can interpret it; and I have heard it said about you, that when you hear a dream you can interpret it." 16 Joseph then answered Pharaoh, saying, "It is not in me; God will give Pharaoh a favorable answer." 39 So Pharaoh said to Joseph, "Since God has informed you of all this, there is no one so discerning and wise as you are. 40 You shall be over my house, and according to your command all my people shall do homage; only in the throne I will be greater than you." 41 Pharaoh said to Joseph, "See, I have set you over all the land of Egypt."

Genesis 50:19-20

19 But Joseph said to them, "Do not be afraid, for am I in God's place? 20 As for you, you meant evil against me, *but* God meant it for good in order to bring about this present result, to preserve many people alive."

Discussion Questions

1. Who was Jacob and what is the significance of his 12 sons? What other name was Jacob given?

2. Through which of Jacob's sons did Jesus descend? What did Levi and his descendants do?

3. Who was Joseph and what did his brothers do to him?

4. How did God work through the tragedy in Joseph's life and end up blessing his family in the process?

5. What ended up happening to the Jews while they were in Egypt?

NOTES

_____

_____

_____

_____

_____

_____

_____

_____

_____

_____

_____

_____

_____

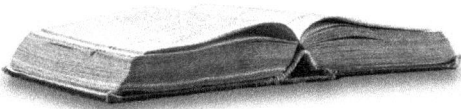

CHAPTER 7

Moses and The Exodus

Out of the generations of enslaved Israelites (also called Hebrews) would come one man, Moses, who would lead them out of Egypt, fulfilling God's divine plan. This was the "Exodus." For over 400 years, they had been away from the Promised Land. God had shown His power through Moses to the Egyptian Pharaoh by sending 10 plagues, each one more severe than the last. These plagues finally persuaded Pharaoh to let the Israelites go back to their homeland. The last plague, one of death to the firstborn, would "pass over" the Israelites but break the Pharaoh's stubbornness. His own son fell to the curse of death and he finally let them go. From this event, God established an annual remembrance called "Passover."

On their journey, they were chased by Egyptian soldiers and encountered the Red Sea which would have to be crossed. The sea was parted by God, and the Israelites passed through on dry ground. However, Pharaoh's men did not; they were covered by a wall of water. The Israelites proceeded on a desert journey that would take them 40 years to complete because of their unfaithfulness. God kept that generation from entering the Promised Land, but provided for their needs while in the desert. During this time, the Tabernacle was constructed so they could worship God. It was a structure, designed by God himself, that the Israelites could take with them wherever they went. God led them as a pillar of cloud by day and as a pillar of fire by night. This was also the time that God gave Moses and the Israelites the Ten Commandments.

Exodus 12:21-22

21 Then Moses called for all the elders of Israel and said to them, "Go and take for yourselves lambs according to your families, and slay the Passover lamb. 22 You shall take a bunch of hyssop and dip it in the blood which is in the basin, and apply some of the blood that is in the basin to the lintel and the two doorposts; and none of you shall go outside the door of his house until morning."

Exodus 14:21-22

21 Then Moses stretched out his hand over the sea; and the Lord swept the sea *back* by a strong east wind all night and turned the sea into dry land, so the waters were divided. 22 The sons of Israel went through the midst of the sea on the dry land, and the waters *were like* a wall to them on their right hand and on their left.

Exodus 13:21-22

21 The Lord was going before them in a pillar of cloud by day to lead them on the way, and in a pillar of fire by night to give them light, that they might travel by day and by night. 22 He did not take away the pillar of cloud by day, nor the pillar of fire by night, from before the people.

Discussion Questions

1. Who was Moses and what did he do? How long were the Jews in Egypt?

2. What other names are associated with the Jews?

3. What did God do to finally break the yoke of slavery for His people?

4. What does the word "Passover" mean?

5. How were the Israelites able to cross the Red Sea, but the Egyptian soldiers were not? How long were they in the desert and what all happened to them while there? Why were they in the desert so long, and unable to enter the Promised Land of Israel?

NOTES

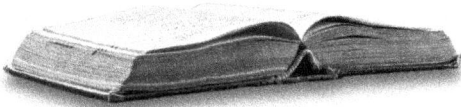

CHAPTER 8

Return to The Promised Land

As this generation of unfaithful Israelites passed away, God finally allowed the Jews to enter the Promised Land. Even with the return to their homeland, they did not always obey God. As a result, there were long periods of years when they were in turmoil. It was during this time that the Judges and Kings became a part of the history of the Israelites. King David is one of the best known kings, and it is through him and the tribe of Judah, that Jesus descended.

One of the nations of the region was Babylon, which is today known as Iraq. Because of Israel's disobedience, God allowed Babylon to conquer Israel and take them captive. It was during this time that the prophets Daniel, Jeremiah and Ezekiel did most of their writing. In particular, the prophecies of Daniel were written during the Babylonian captivity.

As time moved on, other empires rose to power. Daniel prophesied that the Medes and Persians (Iran) would rule the world, then the Greeks (300 BC), and finally the Romans (100 BC). All of these prophecies came true. The Romans became great conquerors and one of their greatest achievements was the building of roads. Jesus came at the precise time to fulfill God's plan. Now, with the construction of the Roman roads to the provinces, the *Good News* could truly be spread throughout the land.

Daniel 9:11

Indeed all Israel has transgressed Your law and turned aside, not obeying Your voice; so the curse has been poured out on us, along with the oath which is written in the law of Moses the servant of God, for we have sinned against Him.

Genesis 49:10

The scepter shall not depart from Judah, Nor the ruler's staff from between his feet, Until Shiloh comes, And to him shall be the obedience of the peoples.

Daniel 8:20-21

20 The ram which thou sawest having two horns are the kings of Media and Persia. 21 And the rough goat is the king of Grecia: and the great horn that is between his eyes is the first king.

Discussion Questions

1. Who was one of the best-known kings in Jewish history, and who descended from him?

2. How did God deal with Israel for their disobedience? What country took them captive? What name is this country known by today?

3. What prophets spoke for God during the Babylonian captivity?

4. After Babylon, what other countries rose to power? Who prophesied years in advance that this would happen?

5. Rome was in power during Jesus' life. What did they do that allowed the *Good News* of Jesus to spread throughout the land?

NOTES

_____

_____

_____

_____

_____

_____

_____

_____

_____

_____

_____

_____

_____

CHAPTER 9

John the Baptist

John the Baptist was a relative of Jesus. His mother, Elizabeth, and the mother of Jesus, Mary, were most likely cousins. John was a prophet who served to light the way to Jesus. Before Jesus' ministry began, John was preaching in the wilderness (desert). His message was one of repentance, for the Kingdom of God was at hand. People came to him to repent of their sins and be baptized in the Jordan River. He preached that One greater than him would soon be coming.

Then one day, Jesus appeared among the crowd to be baptized by John. John told Jesus that he should be baptized by Him instead. Jesus insisted that this must be done to fulfill scripture, so John obeyed. At this event, the Trinity was on display. The Holy Spirit descended in the form of a dove and came to rest on Jesus, while the Father's voice from Heaven said, "This is my beloved Son, in whom I am well-pleased." On that day, the physical senses could see and hear the Father, Son and Holy Spirit.

Jesus was now on the Earth to proclaim the *Good News* of the Bible to all who would listen, turn to Him in faith, and receive eternal life. After Jesus' ministry increased, the ministry of John decreased. He was imprisoned by King Herod, and was later beheaded.

Matthew 3:1-2

1 Now in those days John the Baptist came, preaching in the wilderness of Judea, saying, 2 "Repent for the kingdom of heaven is at hand."

Matthew 3:5-6

5 Then Jerusalem was going out to him, and all Judea and all the district around the Jordan; 6 and they were being baptized by him in the Jordan River, as they confessed their sins.

Matthew 3:11

"As for me, I baptize you with water for repentance, but He who is coming after me is mightier than I, and I am not fit to remove His sandals; He will baptize you with the Holy Spirit and fire."

Matthew 3:16-17

16 After being baptized, Jesus came up immediately from the water; and behold the heavens were opened, and he saw the Spirit of God descending as a dove and lighting on Him, 17 and behold a voice out of the heavens said, "This is My beloved Son, in whom I am well-pleased."

Discussion Questions

1. Who was John the Baptist, and how were he and Jesus related?

2. Where did John the Baptist preach and what was his message?

3. Who came one day seeking John's baptism and why was this necessary?

4. Describe the moment the Trinity (Father, Son and Holy Spirit) was on full display.

5. What was the ultimate fate of John the Baptist?

NOTES

_____

_____

_____

_____

_____

_____

_____

_____

_____

_____

_____

_____

_____

_____

CHAPTER 10

Jesus the Christ

Jesus Christ came to Earth at the appointed time. His birth, life, death and resurrection—the divine plan from the heart of God—allows us to be brought back into a relationship with God. It was no accident that Jesus was born at the time he was. Our God is a God of love and justice. God's love for us needed a "just" way to forgive our sins. Christ came to pay the penalty of death for sin in our place, allowing us to be in right-standing with God. Adam was created with a spirit that was alive and in relationship with God; but when his free will was tested, he chose to disobey God. His relationship with God was broken and Adam became "spiritually dead," or separated from God.

Jesus is the only person other than Adam to ever be born spiritually alive. All who came after Adam, but lived before the resurrection of Jesus, were born and remained "spiritually dead" until Jesus paid the penalty for their sins. Jesus was the only one who could make us spiritually alive again. Because His Father is God and not Man (*this is why the virgin birth is essential*), Jesus was not a descendant of Adam, thereby breaking the cycle. With Adam's sin, all that came after him (except Jesus) were born spiritually dead because the sin nature was passed on by their earthly father. Through the sacrifice of Jesus we are forgiven and become spiritually alive when we accept Him as our Savior. Jesus is called the "Second Adam" because He reversed the act of Adam's disobedience in the Garden. Jesus is both fully human and fully God. There is no one like Him in all of history. He was the only one who could pay the penalty for all our sins.

To be acceptable to God, we have to be totally without sin, that is, perfect. God doesn't grade on a curve. It's not about your good deeds outweighing your bad . It's not about "works"; we can't earn our way into heaven. Good works are not the required payment for eternal life with God. It's not a matter of big sins versus little sins. God's standard is no sins at all, ever (thought, word, or deed). So, how can anyone ever be acceptable to God? We can't, and that's why we need a Savior. Jesus is the only person who has ever lived without any sin. So, God took care of the sin problem for us because we couldn't do it ourselves. Yes, we need a Savior and His name is Jesus!

Romans 5:6

For while we were still helpless, at the right time Christ died for the ungodly.

John 3:16

For God so loved the world, that He gave His only begotten Son, that whoever believes in Him shall not perish, but have eternal life.

Romans 5:12

Therefore, just as through one man sin entered into the world, and death through sin, and so death spread to all men, because all sinned.

John 14:6

Jesus said to him, "I am the way, and the truth, and the life; no one comes to the Father but through Me."

Discussion Questions

1. What was God's plan to allow us to be brought back into a right relationship with Him?

2. When Adam sinned, he became spiritually dead. What does this mean? So, why do we sin? Why is the virgin birth so essential? So, who is Jesus' Father?

3. Doesn't God grade on a curve? What if my good works outweigh my bad? Don't my good works count for anything?

4. Why is Jesus the only way to God? Aren't there many ways to be right with God? What about the Jews, Muslims, Hindus, Buddhists?

5. If you were standing at the gates of Heaven and were asked why you should be let in, what would you say; and what is the right answer?

NOTES

CHAPTER 11

The Holy Spirit

Jesus was alive on the Earth for about 33 years and His ministry was only about three years long. Before He ascended to Heaven, Jesus said He would send another Helper to us: the Holy Spirit. Jesus was only one person, but the Holy Spirit was everywhere and would come to live inside each person who accepted Jesus and became spiritually alive. He said the Holy Spirit would be our Comforter and that He would teach us and lead us into all truth and understanding.

In the Old Testament, the Holy Spirit was present but He couldn't live "inside" anyone because all were spiritually dead. All the Holy Spirit could do was to be "upon" a person chosen by God for a special assignment, such as one of the Old Testament prophets. God selectively and temporarily empowered them with the Holy Spirit, but at an event in the New Testament called Pentecost, the Holy Spirit was given to live inside every believer permanently. When someone says Jesus lives in my heart, this is what they are saying: God is present inside me in the person of the Holy Spirit.

John 14:16-17

16 I will ask the Father, and He will give you another Helper, that He may be with you forever; 17 *that is* the Spirit of truth, whom the world cannot receive, because it does not see Him or know Him, *but* you know Him because He abides with you and will be in you.

John 16:13

But when He, the Spirit of truth, comes, He will guide you into all the truth; for He will not speak on His own initiative, but whatever He hears, He will speak; and He will disclose to you what is to come.

Acts 2:1-4

1 When the day of Pentecost had come, they were all together in one place. 2 And suddenly there came from heaven a noise like a violent rushing wind, and it filled the whole house where they were sitting. 3 And there appeared to them tongues as of fire distributing themselves and they rested on each one of them. 4 And they were all filled with the Holy Spirit and began to speak with other tongues, as the Spirit was giving them utterance.

Discussion Questions

1. Who did Jesus promise to send to us after he was resurrected and left the Earth?

2. Where would the Holy Spirit live, and what would He be sent to do for us?

3. Where was the Holy Spirit during Old Testament times, and why?

4. What happened in the New Testament on the Day of Pentecost?

5. When someone says Jesus lives in my heart, what are they saying?

NOTES

_____

_____

_____

_____

_____

_____

_____

_____

_____

_____

_____

_____

_____

_____

CHAPTER 12

Paul, Peter and the Apostles

After Jesus died and was resurrected to life, He appeared to many people before He ascended to Heaven. Most of these were His closest companions, His disciples (called Apostles), but the Bible also says He appeared to as many as 500 people at one time. He also appeared to a man named Saul on the Road to Damascus, even after He had already ascended to Heaven.

Saul (later called Paul) was a devout Jew and did not believe Jesus was the Messiah (the Christ), so he persecuted the early Christians for their belief. After Paul met Jesus, he became His biggest follower and traveled to many countries to spread the *Good News*. He also wrote the majority of the Bible's New Testament.

Peter wrote several books of the Bible. He and the other Apostles were also responsible for spreading the Gospel of Jesus Christ.

Acts 9:3-5a

**3 As he journeyed he came near Damascus,
and suddenly a light shone around him from
heaven. 4 Then he fell to the ground, and heard
a voice saying to him, "Saul, Saul, why are you
persecuting Me?" 5a And he said, "Who are You,
Lord?" Then the Lord said, "I am Jesus, whom you
are persecuting."**

I Corinthians 15:6

**After that He appeared to more than five hundred
brethren at one time, most of whom remain until
now, but some have fallen asleep.**

Discussion Questions

1. How do we know Jesus was resurrected? How many
people did he appear to at one time?

2. Who was Saul and what did he do before Jesus appeared
to him on the Road to Damascus?

3. What did Paul (formerly called Saul) do after he
personally met Jesus?

4. Who wrote the majority of the Bible's New Testament?
Who wrote several books?

5. Who were the Apostles and what did they do?

CHAPTER 13

The Second Coming

Before Jesus ascended to Heaven, He said He would come again. In the "last days" or "end times," Jesus will return to Earth as the King of Glory. He will gather all the believers to Himself and will judge all the unbelievers. Those who have refused to believe will be judged according to their works, and all will be found guilty because all have sinned. Believers have already been judged at the Cross and Jesus paid our penalty, but unbelievers will have to pay the penalty for themselves. This is not what God wants. He wants all to be saved, but we all have free will and so we must choose which way to go. In the book of Joshua, it says, "Choose this day whom you will serve." And Joshua said, "As for me and my house, we will serve the Lord."

Acts 1:11

They also said, "Men of Galilee, why do you stand looking into the sky? This Jesus, who has been taken up from you into heaven, will come in just the same way as you have watched Him go into heaven."

II Thessalonians 2:1

Now we beseech you, brethren, by the coming of our Lord Jesus Christ, and by our gathering together unto him.

Romans 14:10b-12

10b For we will all stand before the judgment seat of God; 11 for it is written,"As I live, says the Lord, every knee shall bow to me and every tongue shall confess to God." 12 So then each of us will give an account of himself to God.

Revelation 20:12, 15

12 And I saw the dead, the great and the small, standing before the throne, and books were opened; and another book was opened, which is *the book* of life; and the dead were judged from the things which were written in the books, according to their deeds. 15 And if anyone's name was not found written in the book of life, he was thrown into the lake of fire.

Joshua 24:15

If it is disagreeable in your sight to serve the Lord, choose for yourselves today whom you will serve: whether the gods which your fathers served which were beyond the River, or the gods of the Amorites in whose land you are living; but as for me and my house, we will serve the Lord.

Discussion Questions

1. What did Jesus say just before He ascended to Heaven?

2. During what days will He return to Earth and in what manner?

3. By what will unbelievers be judged? What about believers?

4. Who does God want to be saved? How do we know this?

5. So, do you have a choice to make? What will you choose?

NOTES

_____

_____

_____

_____

_____

_____

_____

_____

_____

_____

_____

_____

_____

_____

CHAPTER 14

Conclusion

There are some important questions people have: Does God really exist? Is the Bible really the Word of God? Is the Bible really true? Well, there is an abundance of evidence that God exists and that there had to be a Creator based on the things we see. The more we know about the past, through new discoveries in archeology and the sciences, the more they support the things written in the Bible. There are a multitude of prophecies in the Bible that were written down hundreds, and even thousands, of years before they happened that have all been fulfilled just as the Bible said.

The Bible claims to be the word of truth from the one and only God who created us, everything we see and even things we can't see. It is unlike any other book we will ever read. God is fully capable of speaking to us through its pages. Many people think they know what the Bible says, and may have heard bits and pieces over time, but most have never really read the Bible or studied it for themselves. Deciding for oneself whether the Bible's claims are true is "the most important decision" we will ever be called upon to make in this life... and to not decide is also a decision.

So, if God exists and the Bible is His Word, we can

believe it. He has given us the answers and now all we must do is accept His offer of eternal life through faith. For we have salvation by His Grace alone and not by any of our own works. We all need a Savior, and His name is Jesus. If you have never done so, then right now in prayer, tell God you are ready to accept His great gift. You can certainly just put this prayer in your own words, or you can go to the next chapter, *Prayer To Receive Christ*. If you will do this, it will be the best decision of your life... your eternal life!

Romans 1:19-20

19 For what can be known about God is plain to them, because God has shown it to them. 20 For his invisible attributes, namely, his eternal power and divine nature, have been clearly perceived, ever since the creation of the world, in the things that have been made. So they are without excuse.

Ephesians 2:8-9

8 For by grace you have been saved through faith; and that not of yourselves, *it is* the gift of God; 9 not as a result of works, so that no one may boast.

Hebrews 11:6

And without faith it is impossible to please *Him*, for he who comes to God must believe that He is and *that* He is a rewarder of those who seek Him.

I John 5:11-13

11 And the testimony is this, that God has given us eternal life, and this life is in His Son. 12 He who has the Son has the life; he who does not have the Son of God does not have the life.13 These things I have written to you who believe in the name of the Son of God, so that you may know that you have eternal life.

Discussion Questions

1. How do we know God exists?

2. How do we know the Bible is true and is God's Word to us?

3. What did God do so that we could be reconciled to Him?

4. What makes us right with God, and what must we do to accept His offer of reconciliation?

5. Eternal life begins the moment we accept Jesus as our Lord and Savior. How will you spend eternity?

NOTES

_____

_____

_____

_____

_____

_____

_____

_____

_____

_____

_____

_____

_____

CHAPTER 15

Prayer To Receive Christ

Lord Jesus, I believe in You and ask You to forgive my sins and save me from eternal separation from God. By faith, I accept Your work and death on the cross as sufficient payment for my sins. There is nothing I can add to your finished work. Thank You for providing the way for me to know You and have eternal life. Thank You also for hearing my prayers and loving me unconditionally. Please walk with me and help me fulfill Your plans for me. In Your Name I pray, Amen.

Romans 10:9-10

9 that if you confess with your mouth Jesus as Lord, and believe in your heart that God raised Him from the dead, you will be saved; 10 for with the heart a person believes, resulting in righteousness, and with the mouth he confesses, resulting in salvation.

Appendix

We Need a Savior

And His name is…

JESUS!

God has given us the "gift" of eternal life.

We can never earn it…

For the wages of sin is death, but the free gift of God is eternal life in Christ Jesus our Lord.

-Romans 6:23

For by grace you have been saved through faith; and that not of yourselves, it is the gift of God; not as a result of works, so that no one may boast.

-Ephesians 2:8-9

We can never be "good enough" to save ourselves...

For all have sinned, and fall short of the glory of God.

-Romans 3:23

There is no one who does good, not even one.

-Psalm 14:3b

Jesus is the Savior, the only Savior...

Therefore there is now no condemnation for those who are in Christ Jesus.

-Romans 8:1

And there is salvation in no one else; for there is no other name under heaven that has been given among men by which we must be saved.

-Acts 4:12

So that at the name of Jesus EVERY KNEE WILL BOW, of those who are in heaven and on earth and under the earth, and that every tongue will confess that Jesus Christ is Lord, to the glory of God the Father.

-Philippians 2:10-11

The "world" may tell us there are other ways to be saved, but do not believe it…

See to it that no one takes you captive through philosophy and empty deception, according to the tradition of men, according to the elementary principles of the world, rather than according to Christ.

-Colossians 2:8

Jesus said to him, "I am the way, and the truth, and the life; no one comes to the Father but through Me".

-John 14:6

Accepting your Savior is simple. God has made it easy. You can do it right now…

That if you confess with your mouth Jesus as Lord, and believe in your heart that God raised Him from the dead, you will be saved; for with the heart a person believes, resulting in righteousness, and with the mouth he confesses, resulting in salvation.

-Romans 10:9-10

JESUS LOVES YOU!

About the Authors

At an early age, Al and Jere Litchenburg both accepted Jesus as their Lord and Savior.

Throughout their lives, they have actively attended church, studied the Bible, and taught Sunday School classes. They decided to share what they had learned over the years and created *The Big Picture* to give an overview of the Bible in a clear and concise way. In writing it, their hope was that this short study of the Bible might help people understand God's plan to restore His relationship with mankind after it was lost in the Garden of Eden.

They believe that if people know the "big picture," they can be inspired to read the Bible on their own, to understand that through Jesus our relationship with God has been restored, and to discover all the great things God has done... just because He loves us!

Al and Jere first met in junior high, dated during high school and have now been married for 53 years. They have a loving and growing family and were blessed to have them write the Foreword for this book!

For additional information, see the online version at:

www.bible-bigpicture.com

What Questions Does
The Big Picture Answer?

1. If God is love, why won't he just let all of us into heaven? (p. 15, 53)

2. How old is the Earth? What does science say, and what does the Bible say? (p. 18)

3. When did Jesus come into being? (p. 18)

4. How should we interpret the Bible? (p. 21)

5. Why did God create us with free will? (p. 21)

6. Who tempted Adam and Eve to sin? (p. 22)

7. Where in the Bible is the first promise of a Savior? (p. 25)

8. Why did God destroy so many people in the Flood? (p. 29)

9. Why was Abraham willing to sacrifice his son, Isaac? (p. 33)

10. Why do we sin? (p. 53)

11. Doesn't God grade on a curve? What if my good works outweigh my bad? (p. 54)

12. Why is Jesus the only way to God? Aren't there many ways to be right with God? What about the Jews, Muslims, Hindus, Buddhists? (p. 53-54)

13. Why is the virgin birth so essential? (p. 53)

14. Don't my good works count for anything? (p. 54)

15. If you were standing at the gates of Heaven and were asked why you should be let in, what would you say; and what is the right answer? (p. 54)

16. How do we know Jesus was resurrected? (p. 61)

17. Is Jesus coming back to judge us? When? (p. 63)

18. How do we know God exists? (p. 67)

19. How do we know the Bible is true and is God's Word to us? (p. 67)

20. What must we do to be saved? (p. 67, 71)

NOTES

_____

_____

_____

_____

_____

_____

_____

_____

_____

_____

_____

_____

_____

_____

NOTES

_____

_____

_____

_____

_____

_____

_____

_____

_____

_____

_____

_____

_____

The Big Picture: Restoration of Relationship

www.ingramcontent.com/pod-product-compliance
Lightning Source LLC
Chambersburg PA
CBHW070553030426
42337CB00016B/2477